CONTENTS

Practice Pages

INTRODUCTION

HISTORY

For some people history is a favorite subject to be savored and for others it is a dreaded subject to be endured. For someone with an interest in learning the art of calligraphy, a look at the history of calligraphy can be fascinating. When did all of this beautiful writing begin? Why was it considered a necessity and not an extravagance to devote endless hours to creating such beauty?

The art of calligraphy is believed to have started with the ancient story-telling pictures that were drawn on the walls of caves. As the human race developed, so did the cave paintings, and around 3500 BC the Egyptians created a form of highly stylized writing called hieroglyphics, which they painted on the walls of the tombs of their nobility. A few thousand years later, around 1000 BC, the Phoenicians created what is believed by scholars to be one of the first alphabets and writing systems. The Phoenicians were seafarers who journeyed to different ports and carried their use of written language with them. It is believed that these Phoenician seafarers influenced the Greeks who later developed their own form of writing. The word *calligraphy* derives from the Greek terms *kallos*, which means "beautiful," and *graphein*, "to write." Throughout the ages, calligraphy has been defined as "beautiful writing."

The Romans learned their writing skills from the Greeks and by 850 BC had

adapted the letters and the words to the Latin language. In the centuries following the fall of the Roman Empire, Latin continued to be the language of the church throughout Europe, and it was through the church that this written language was initially preserved. Because the word of God was considered divine, monks be-

CALLIGRAPHY

BY JO PACKHAM & MATT SHAY

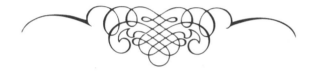

Mud Puddle inc.

NEW YORK

Calligraphy
by Jo Packham and Matt Shay

Copyright © 2009 by Mud Puddle, Inc.

Mud Puddle, Inc.
36 W. 25th Street
New York, NY 10010
info@mudpuddleinc.com

ISBN: 978-160311-202-4

Printed and bound in China

gan to carefully scribe ancient texts into beautifully written and decorated books that were treated with great respect by the clergy and nobility that had access to them. Paper was rare and expensive even for royalty and the church, so the monks developed a style of writing that was condensed, allowing more words to fit on a single line. This style became known as Gothic and was used throughout the Middle Ages.

In the mid-15th century Johannes Gutenberg invented the printing press and developed type based on the Gothic lettering style of the monks. This new technique allowed for faster, less expensive printing, but it threatened the continuation of the ornate work done by the monks. Calligraphers were threatened once again in the 17th century with the advent of copperplate engraving, which permitted the printing of very fine lines similar to italic script. In the mid-19th century, William Morris introduced the flat-edged pen and began a calligraphy revival, bringing back the popular art form of beautiful writing.

It might seem that the art of calligraphy could not possibly withstand the ease and popularity of the computer, but calligraphy is more popular today than ever and is supported by calligraphic societies throughout the world. Calligraphy is both an art form and a type of craft that encompasses the finest, most ornate handwriting as well as highly creative letters and writing styles.

# OOLS & MATERIALS

Expert calligraphers use a wide range of both traditional and innovative products. These include a variety of different types and sizes of nibs, pens, fountain pens, inks, markers, and papers to create the art of writing. However, the beginner needs only a few items and practice time to begin this art and craft form.

TOOLS & MATERIALS FOR BEGINNERS

Markers

Until recently markers were not the best choice for use in calligraphy. The marker end would not hold its edge, which resulted in bleeding letters and lines that were not crisp and clean enough for good calligraphy symbols. Today, however, durable markers with two ends, one that is broad and chiseled and one that is pointed, are available in both water-soluble and permanent inks and a variety of sizes and colors. These calligraphy markers are most often found at art supply stores.

Fountain Pens

Fountain pens are the second easiest tool for beginners to use because you do not have to worry about constantly dipping the pen nib into the inkwell — an aspect of calligraphy that will take a little practice to master. Fountain pens supply ink through a cartridge that automatically controls the ink flow. Cartridges are available in both water-soluble and permanent inks in many colors. The pens are equipped with permanent nibs or interchangeable nibs in several different sizes for both left- and right-handed calligraphers.

Paper

One of the most important materials to be used in calligraphy is the paper — it is mandatory that you use paper that will work successfully with the writing tools and inks you have selected. Before beginning to practice your project, you should test the paper with the marker or pen you will be using. Some papers are difficult to work on, some "bleed" (cause the ink to spread), some have a texture that interferes with the writing tool, and some have shiny coated surfaces that cause the ink to bead on the paper surface. Beginners should begin practice with an economical layout bond paper.

Additional Tools & Materials

1. Drawing board
2. Newsprint paper or paper pads that cushion your writing paper (see How to Begin)
3. Large paper clips
4. Protractor
5. Practice paper

TOOLS & MATERIALS FOR INTERMEDIATE CALLIGRAPHERS

Dip Pens

A dip pen with interchangeable nibs is the more traditional calligraphy pen. Nibs are available both broad-edged and pointed and are inserted into the end of the penholder. You select your nib type depending on the calligraphy style lettering you are planning.

To load the ink, dip the nib into an inkwell or bottle and then begin writing. The ink flows off the pen nib as you write, and then at some point you must stop and dip your pen back into the ink. It takes practice to keep the ink flow consistent and to prevent the ink from dripping onto the paper after you reload the nib.

Inks

Pigmented acrylic inks manufactured today are either water-soluble or permanent and are archival. They are available in most art supply stores in a large variety of rich, intense colors. As you advance in your calligraphy skills, you will want to learn to control the opacity of your inks by grinding Chinese stick ink into your inks. For color work, you can learn to use gouache (a type of watercolor and chalk).

Brushes

Brushes used for calligraphy are either pointed or flat. Art supply stores carry a wide variety of sizes. The brush bristles can be synthetic or made of animal hair. Intermediate calligraphers should start with flat lettering brushes with short chisel-shaped hair. As your skills progress, you can try pointed brushes for lettering. With a quality brush, you should be able to keep a good point. Sable brushes are the most durable but also the most expensive.

Paper

Smooth or vellum surface bristol board or high-quality machine-made or hand-made paper can be used. Remember to test the paper with your pens and inks before you actually begin your project.

Additional Tools & Materials

1. Good lighting
2. Small transparent T-square metal ruler with a cork back to prevent slipping while measuring
3. Small container of water and paper towels for cleaning nibs

alligraphic glossary

alignment Lining up letters or rows of letters in a straight line from left to right or top to bottom.

angle The slant of the pen or marker to the paper.

anticlockwise The direction of the curved stroke used to make a letter that moves the opposite way to a clock's hands, as in u.

arch The curved section of a lowercase (minuscule) letter that begins from the basic part of the letter, as in h.

arm The horizontal section of a letter, as in z. The letter v has no arms.

ascender The section of a lowercase (minuscule) letter that rises above the waist line, as in h.

ascender line The guideline on the paper that shows the height of the ascender section of the letter.

axis The imaginary vertical or horizontal center line of a letter, as in Q.

base line The writing line that is used as a guide to set all letters on. (see guide lines)

body height The height of the main part of a lowercase (minuscule) letter that does not have sections that rise above the waist line (ascenders) or go below the base line (descenders).

bold A heavier way of writing a word, e.g., **bold**.

Bowl **bowl** The curved part of the letter that surrounds the enclosed negative space (counter), as in b.

branch The first curved part of a letter that is connected to the vertical line (stem) of the letter, as in h.

branching stroke The stroke that joins the first curved part of a letter to the basic vertical line (downstroke) of a letter.

built-up letters Letters that have been created by using additional calligraphy font strokes that are not a basic part of the main calligraphy font.

calligraphy The art or style of beautiful writing. Taken from the Greek *kaligraphia*, from *kallos*, meaning "beauty," and *graphein*, "to write."

cap lines The lines drawn on the practice paper that show the height of the capital (majuscule) letters. (see guide lines)

character Any single letter, number, or unit used in any style or type of lettering, writing, or typing.

composition The organization, design, or layout of letters, graphics, or other materials such as photography on a page or a section of a page.

condensed A series of letters or words that have been moved closer together vertically and sometimes made taller or moved together horizontally.

construction The basic strokes used in the proper order and direction while creating calligraphy letters. The letter F has three strokes.

counter The enclosed empty space inside a letter, as in D.

crossbar A separate horizontal line or stroke in a letter, as in t.

descender The section of a lowercase (minuscule) letter that is made below the base line, as in p.

descender line The guideline on the paper that shows the lowest point of the descender section of the letter.

diagonal The slanted line or stroke in a letter, as in N.

downstroke A line made with a calligraphy stroke that moves down toward the base line or descender line, as in Z or y.

Ductus

ductus The number of, direction of, and order of lines or strokes that are made when writing a calligraphy letter.

flamed stroke A straight or curved line or stroke in a calligraphy letter that is thicker.

flourish A decorative embellishment or extension that is the last addition to a calligraphy letter.

guide lines Lines drawn on the practice paper to indicate where different lines and strokes of the letters should be drawn. Base lines, capital lines, waist lines, ascender lines and descender lines are examples of guide lines.

hairline The finest line that can be produced by a marker or pen.

illuminated calligraphy letters Uppercase (majuscule) letters that are decorated more ornately than other uppercase letters in the body of text.

inverted arch The curved part of a lowercase (minuscule) letter that is connected to the vertical line of the letter, as in u.

majuscule A capital, or uppercase, letter.

minuscule A lowercase letter.

nib The point of a pen that is designed to be inserted into a penholder or fountain pen and used to transfer ink to paper.

nib width The width of an individual nib that is the reference point of calligraphy and is used for measuring pen widths.

pen angle The slant at which the pen point meets with the horizontal writing lines.

script Any style of written letters.

Serifs

serif The small detail strokes on the ends of the main strokes of a letter, number, or symbol.

slant The amount a letter slants from the imaginary straight vertical line.

slant line The imaginary vertical lines that indicate the degree of slant desired.

spacing The art of arranging letters and numbers next to each other or above and below each other.

stem The vertical line of a letter.

stroke A movement of a marker or pen.

waist The slim part in the middle of a straight stroke.

waist line The imaginary line that sets the top limits of the x-height of letters or words. (see guide lines)

x-height The space between the base line and the waist line, or the height of a lowercase letter such as s without ascenders or descenders. (see guide lines)

OW TO BEGIN

Beginners may find it easier, though not essential, to practice calligraphy on a writing surface that is somewhat elevated. If you do not have a drawing table to work on, you can purchase a drawing board at your art supply store. A drawing board should be covered with layers of absorbent paper padding and placed on the tabletop in such a manner that it is both steady and comfortable. Hold your paper padding and writing paper in place with large clips on the two upper corners of your board so they will not be in the way while you are practicing your lettering.

Use a calligraphy marker with a wide, flat, chiseled nib. Using only a fine-point or only a flat-point marker will not create the difference between the thin and thick lines that give the letters and numbers their distinctive calligraphic look. Hold the marker in a firm but comfortable grip so that the point is at a 30-degree angle to the writing lines on your paper, aiming up your forearm toward your shoulder. Practice to learn the correct lettering and to achieve control and comfort when using the marker.

A calligraphy stroke has length and width, it takes up more space than a traditional alphabet letter, and it has a top and bottom end as well as two edges. The thickest line or stroke will be the diagonal from top left to bottom right, and the thinnest line or stroke will be from bottom left to top right. The upright and horizontal lines or strokes are the medium between the thickest and the thinnest. Too sharp a marker angle will make the upright strokes too thin, and too shallow an angle will make them too thick. It may help you as a beginner to regularly check your 30-degree marker angle with a protractor.

When first learning calligraphy or when learning a new alphabet, it is better to practice larger so that when a mistake is made, it is easy to see. To do this, enlarge your practice pages until you think the letters will be an easy size to practice and then practice, practice, practice! When you like the look of your letters, copy the practice pages at actual-size and then practice the letters at this size. Next, begin to practice the letters on a plain sheet of paper with no guide lines. Now you are becoming a calligrapher!

Note: Make certain that you are as aware of the spaces between the letters and between the lines as you are of the lines themselves. Correct letter and line spacing is essential in good calligraphy.

Note: Left-handed calligraphers should experiment to find the most comfortable and most successful paper position to achieve the correct pen angle for each different alphabet. Begin working with your drawing board in the same position you put your paper for everyday handwriting and then make adjustments as you begin to create your letters. You may need to adjust repeatedly as you change letters or try new alphabet styles.

Monoline Alphabet

Monoline letters are the simplest letters in calligraphy because they are quickly formed using a single continuous stroke that gives no thin or thick lines. This is the perfect teaching alphabet for calligraphy. Mastering this very basic alphabet will help you make consistent line widths, proper letter heights, and even spacing between the letters and the lines of letters.

After you have mastered the basic monoline alphabet, try changing the thickness of the letter strokes, the slant of your marker, or the size of different or random letters. It will give your lettering a variety of styles and will give you additional practice in pen slants, spacing, and adjusting to different sizes and heights of letters.

ABCDEFGHIJ

KLMNOPQRST

UVWXYZ&

1234567890

abcdefghij

klmnopqrst

uvwxyz

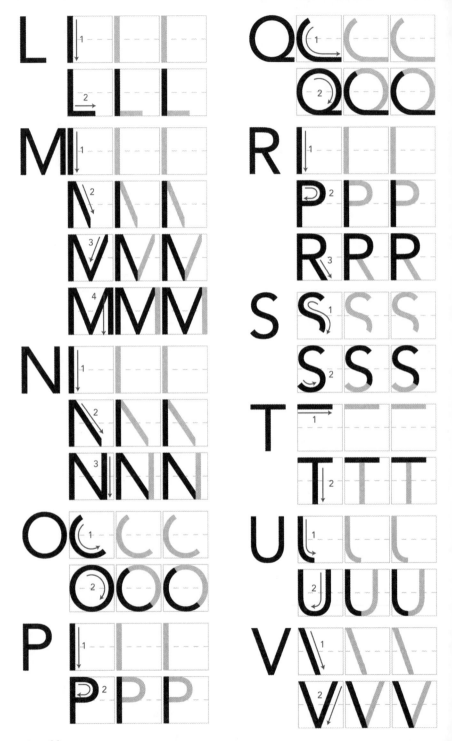

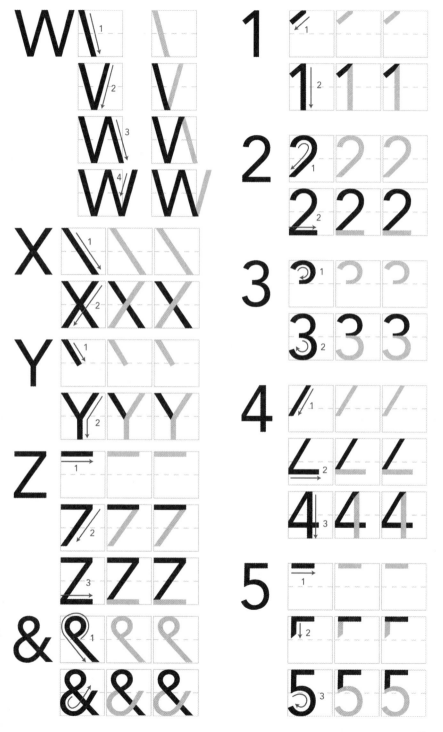

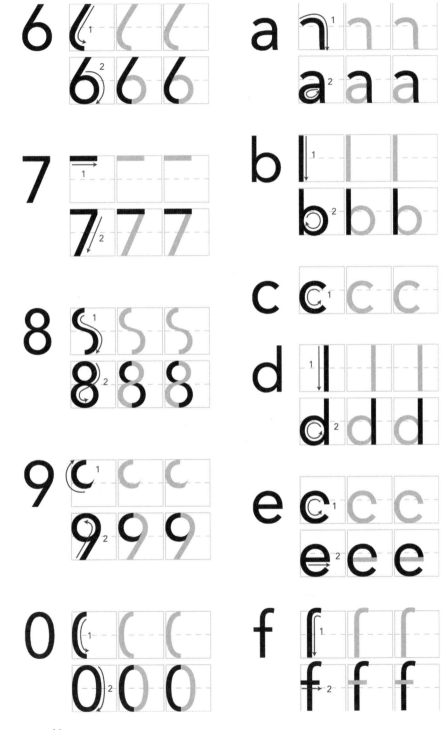

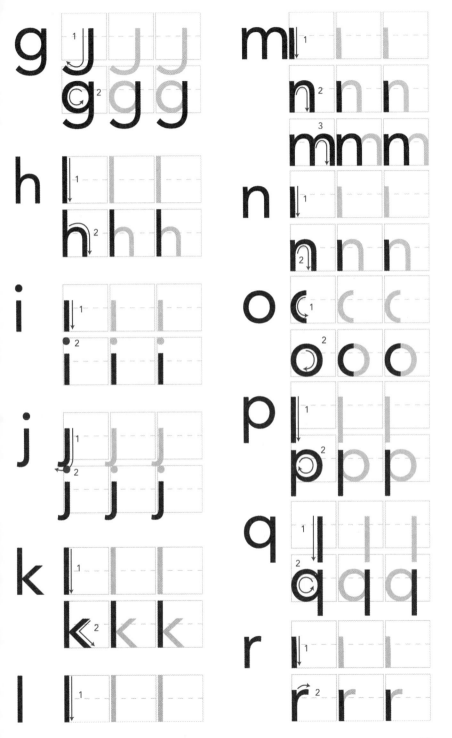

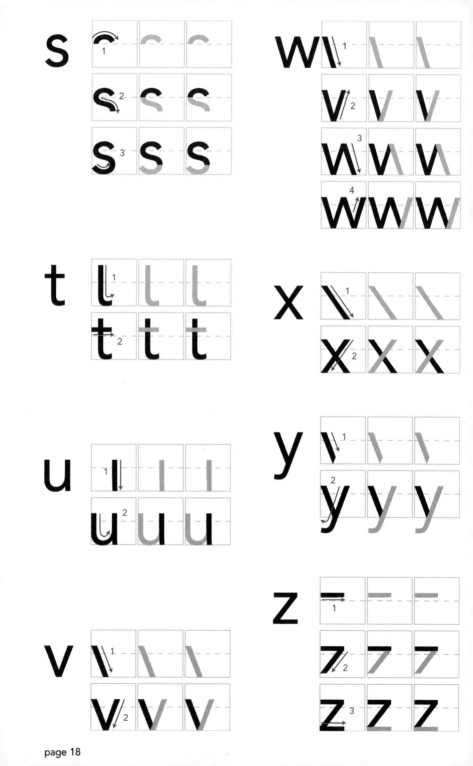

Foundational Hand Alphabet

Edward Johnston, the father of modern calligraphy, developed the Foundational Hand early in the 20th century. He developed this style of lettering based on a classic 10th century form of lettering that had no flourishes. It is the basis for most of the familiar typefaces today, and it was and still remains the lettering style that is used for large calligraphy projects such as re-creating pages of the Bible or other large book manuscripts.

The Foundational Hand was created as only a lowercase (minuscule) alphabet, so in this book Roman capitals are used to add capital (majuscule) letters.

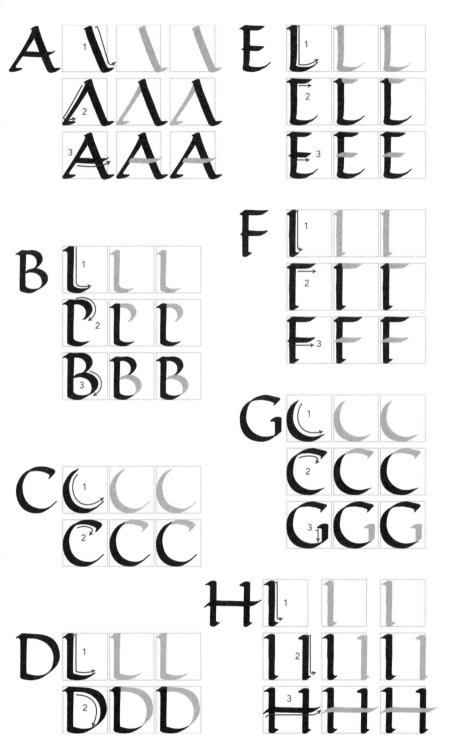

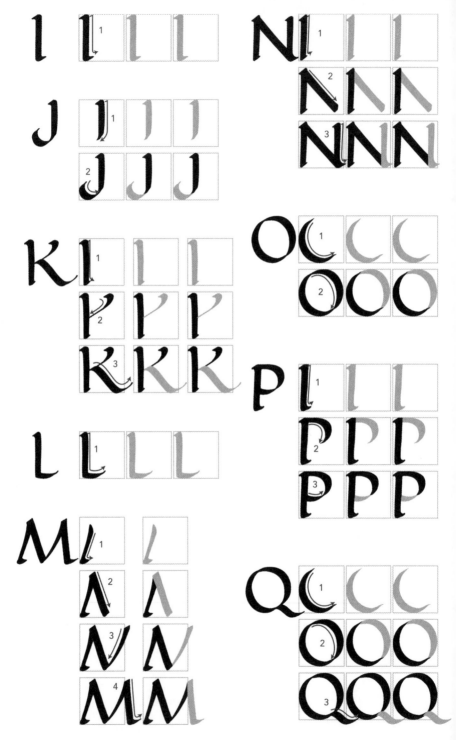

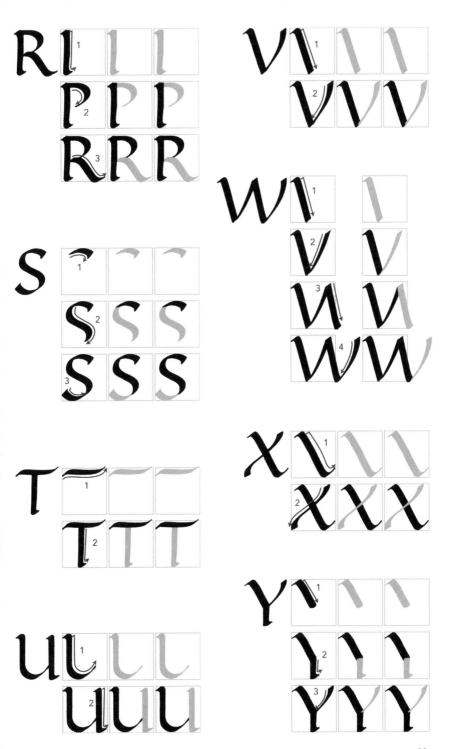

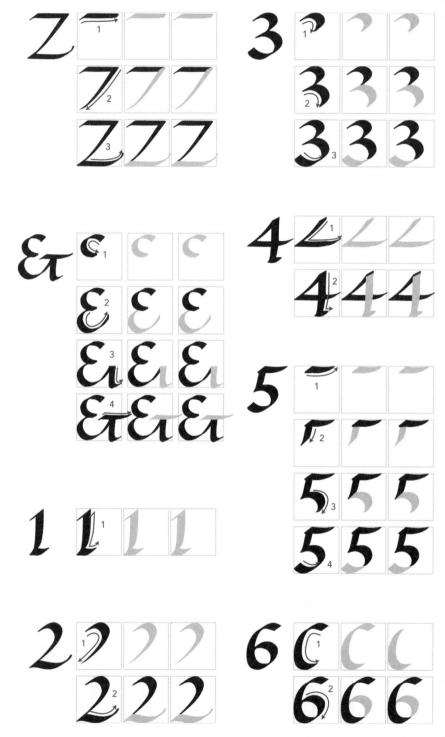

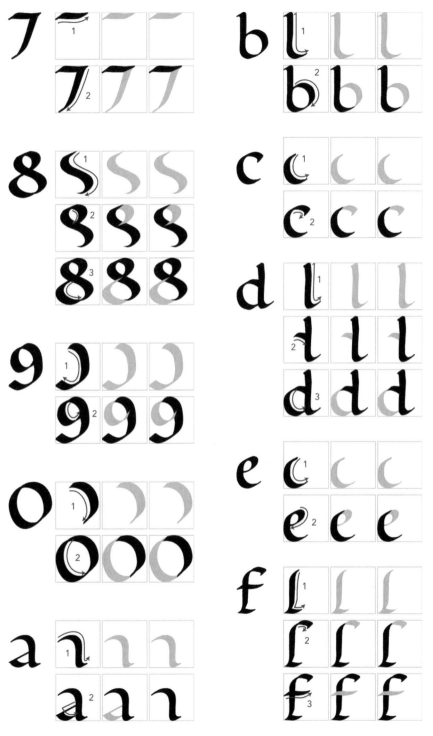

g

h

i

j

k

l

m

n

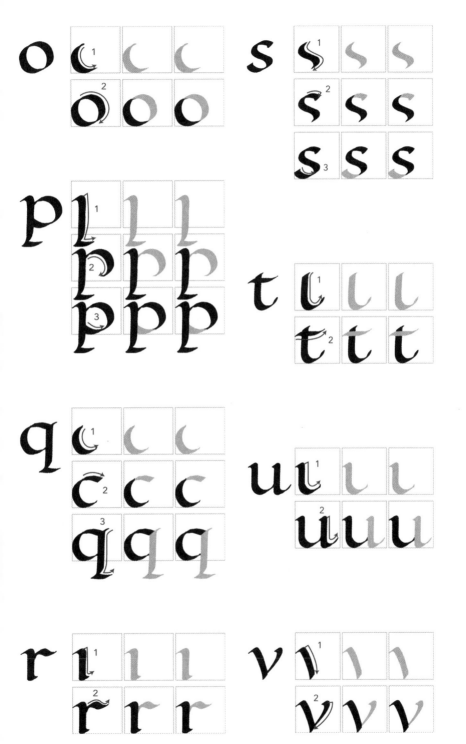

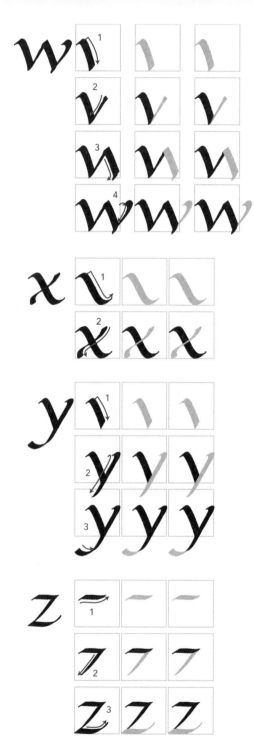

TIMELESS

MOMENTS

quality

Celebrate NIGHTS

Festival

event

Charm

LOOKING

Back

Seasons

BOUNTIFUL

HOLIDAY

sunset NOW

traditional

good

PATIENCE

Forever

special

OCCASIONS

Roman Alphabet

The Roman alphabet is one of the oldest, most important, and widely used alphabetic writing styles in the world today. It is believed to have evolved from the Greek alphabet and was initially developed by the ancient Romans to write the Latin language. Capital Roman letters are widely used because they have perfect geometric proportions.

A B C D E F G H I J
K L M N O P Q R S T
U V W X Y Z &
1 2 3 4 5 6 7 8 9 0
a b c d e f g h i j
k l m n o p q r s t
u v w x y z

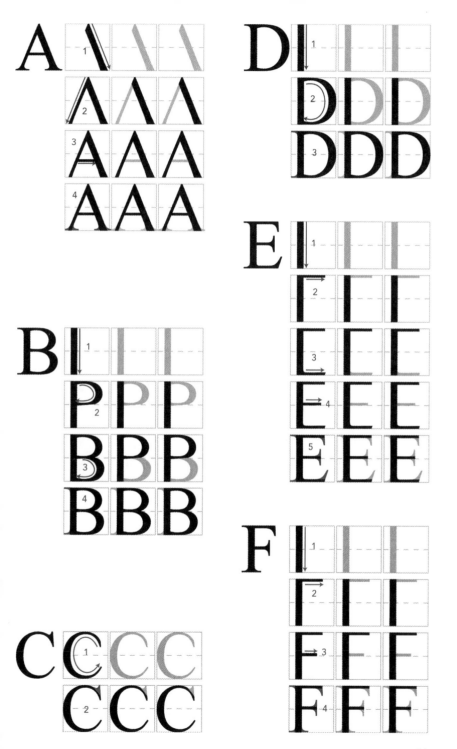

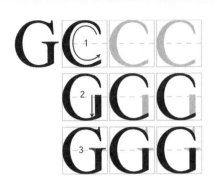

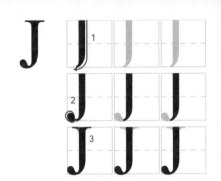

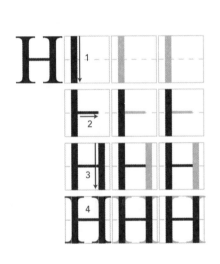

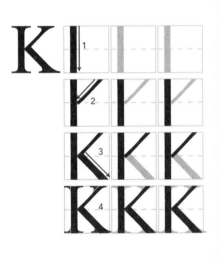

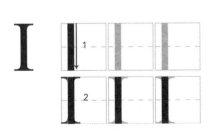

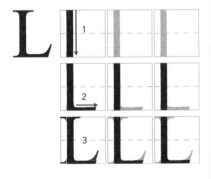

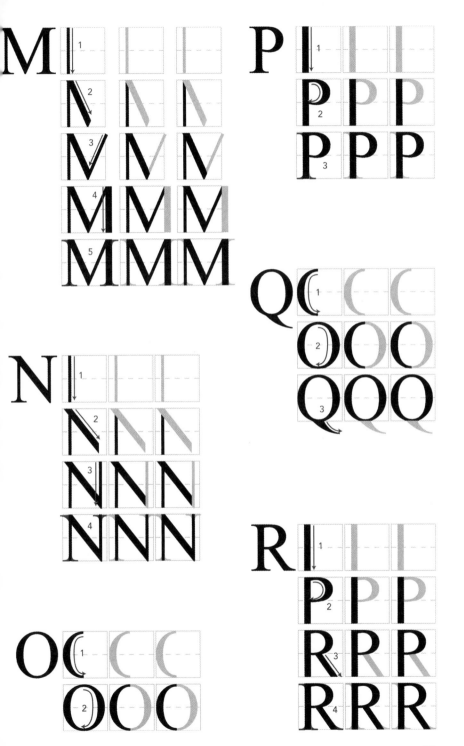

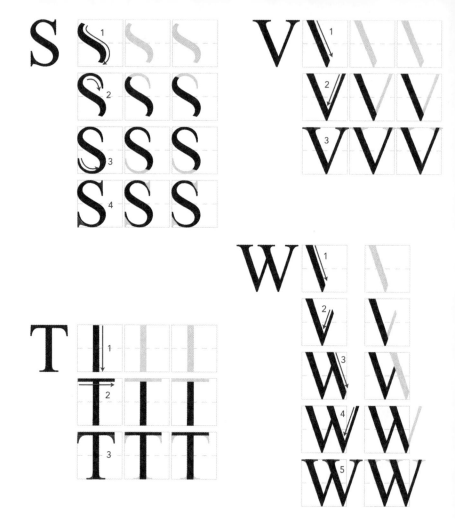

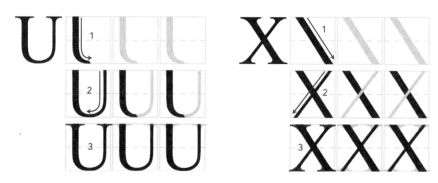

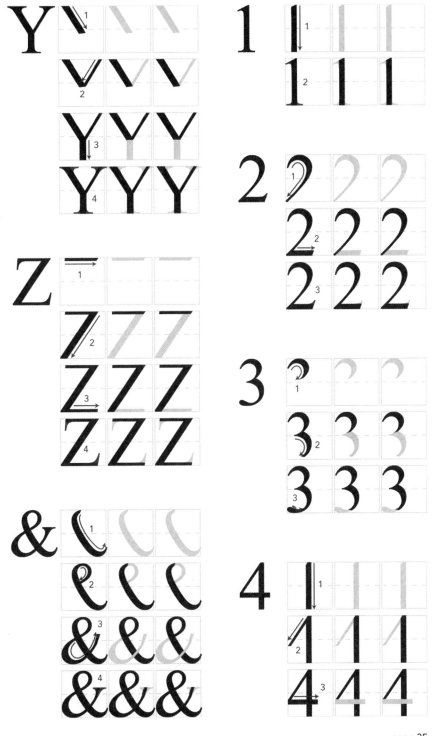

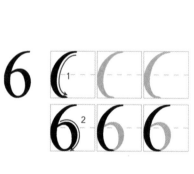

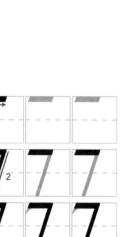

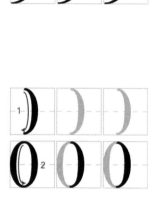

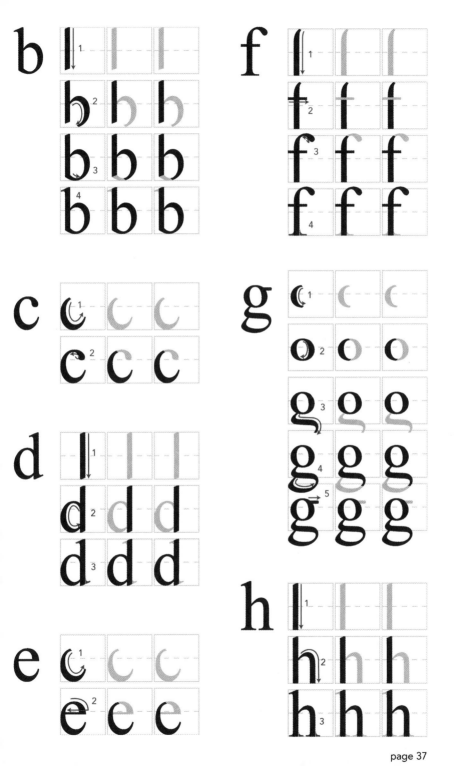

i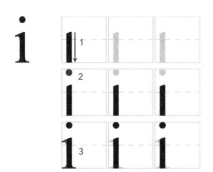

l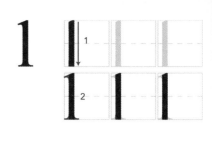

j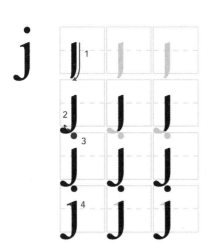

m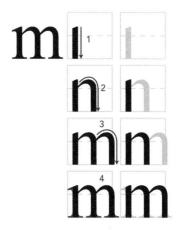

k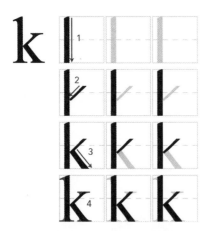

n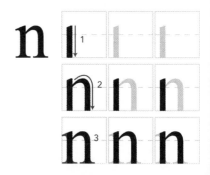

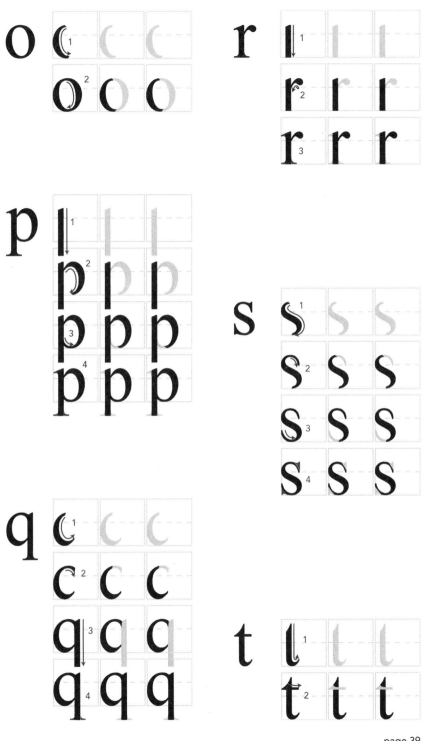

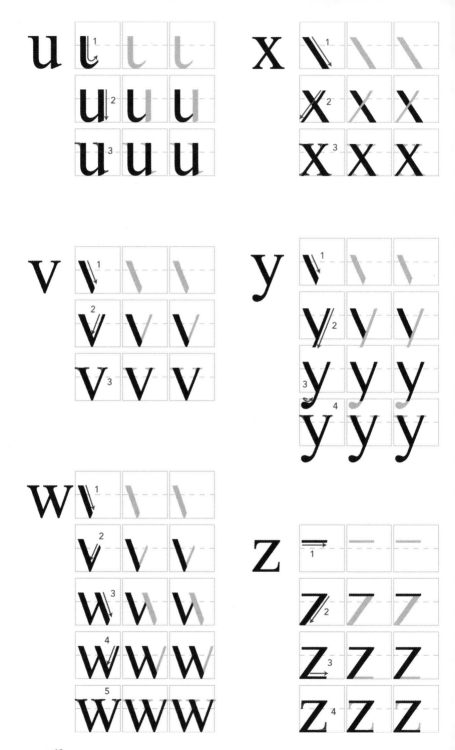

UNCIAL ALPHABET

The ancient Romans were among the first to create calligraphy lettering styles, and their influence spread around the Mediterranean and into Europe. Around 500 AD their writing styles began to emerge in Ireland as uncial script, also referred to as Celtic script. Uncial is a rounded alphabet style with very short ascenders and slight descenders. It has always been used to lend emphasis, such in the titles of manuscripts.

A B C D E F G H I J

K L M N O P Q R S T

U V W X Y Z &

1 2 3 4 5 6 7 8 9 0

a b c d e f g h i j

k l m n o p q r s t

u v w x y z

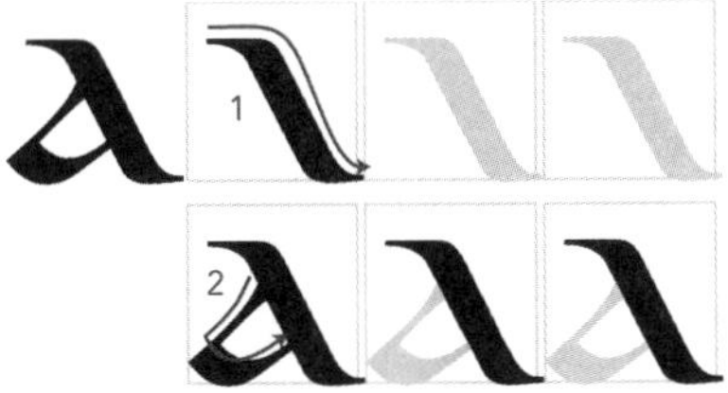

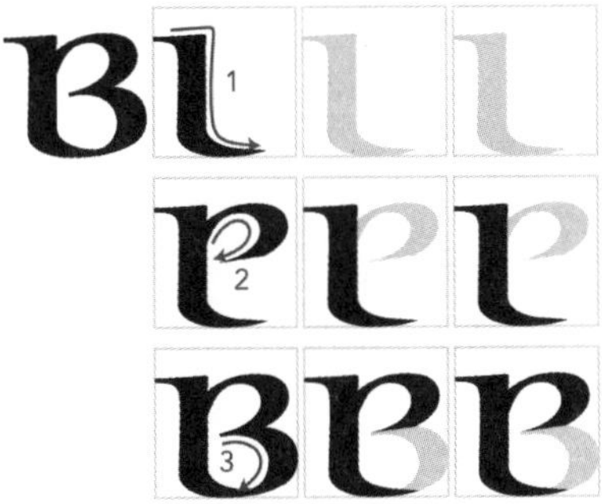

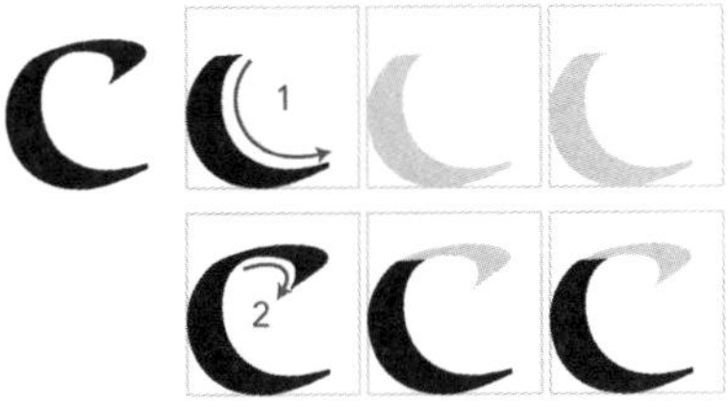

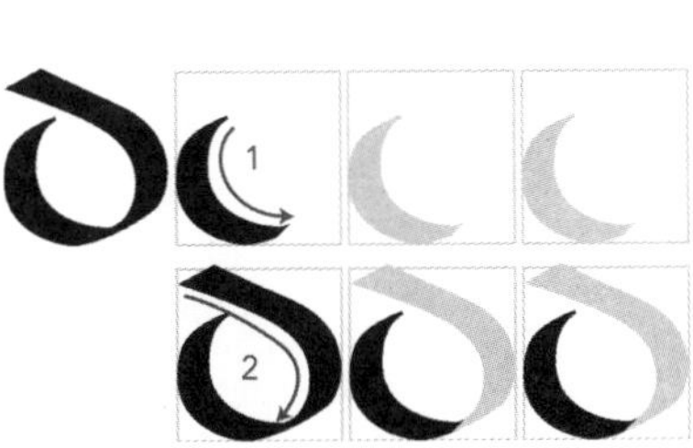

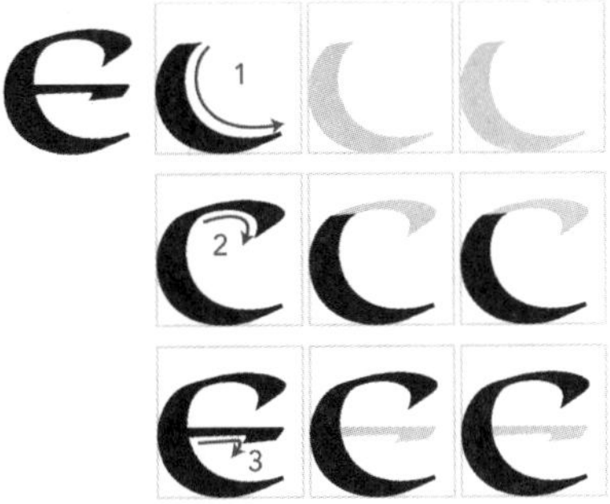

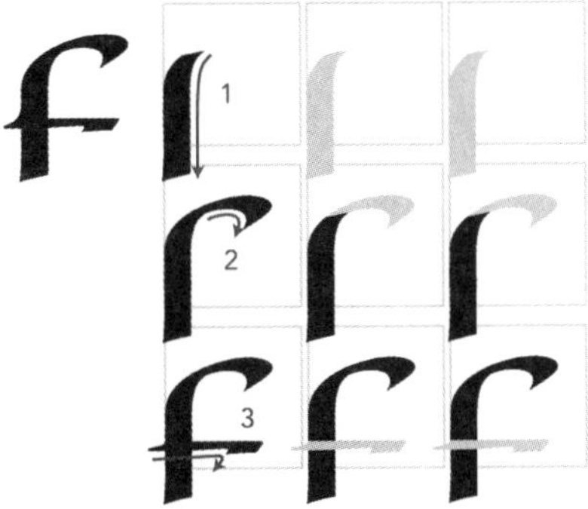

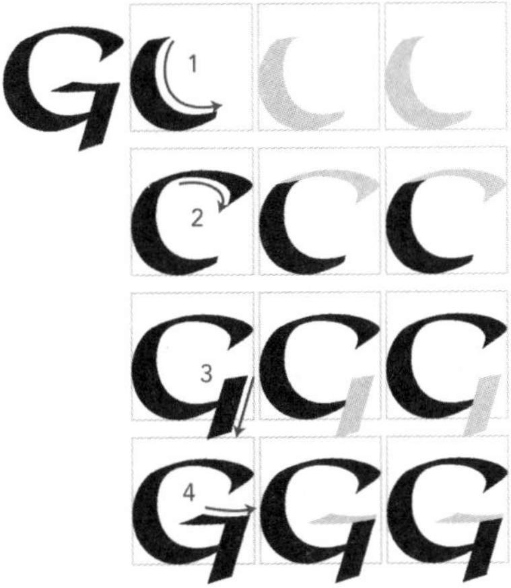

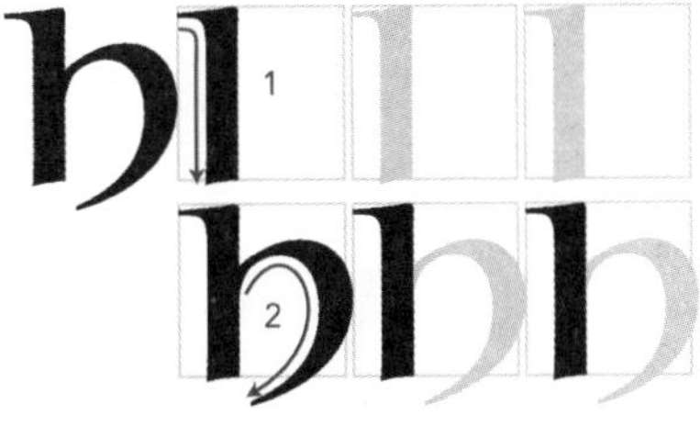

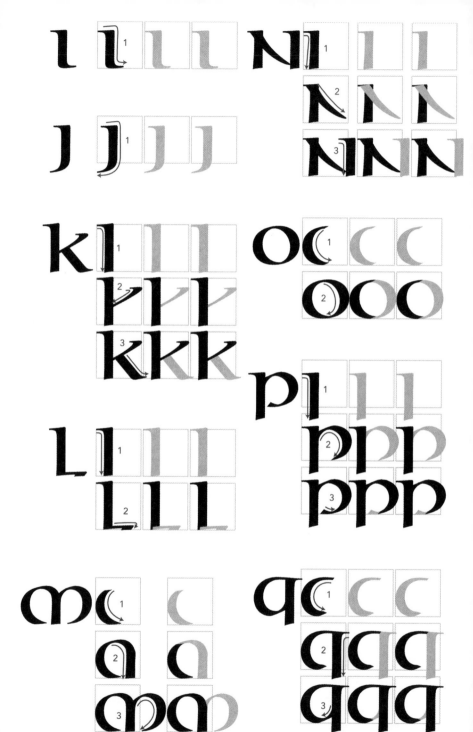

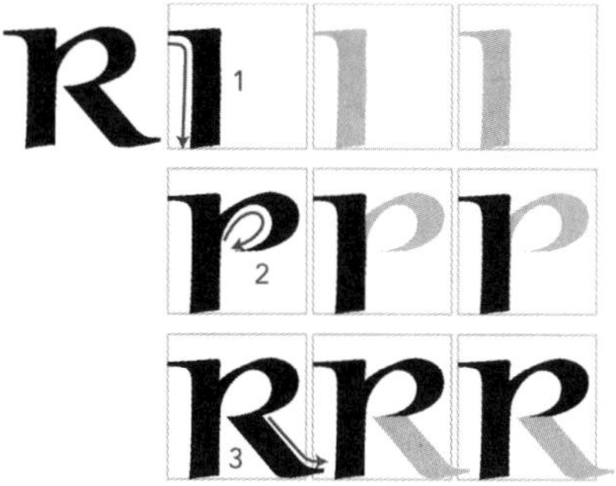

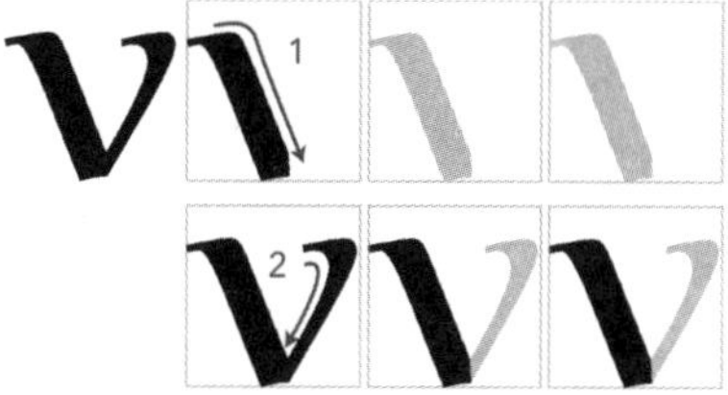

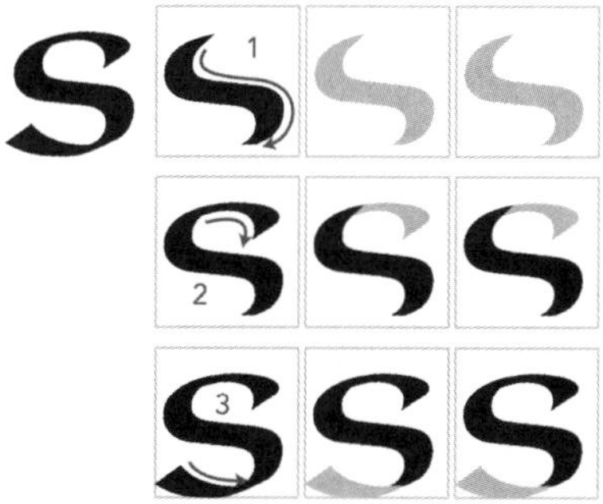

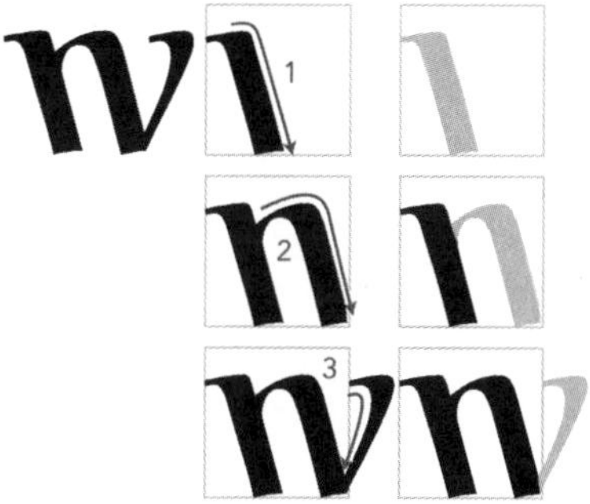

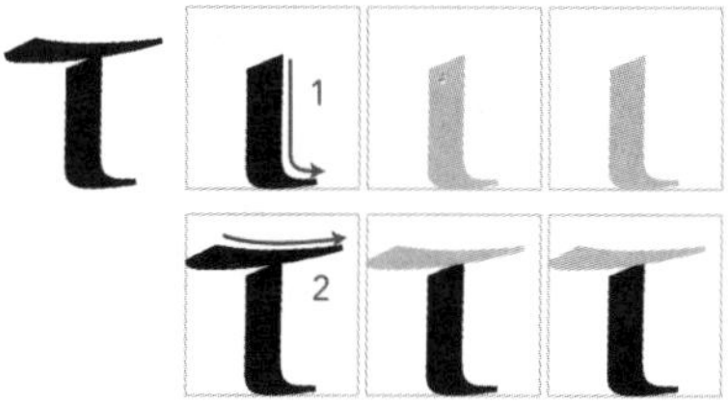

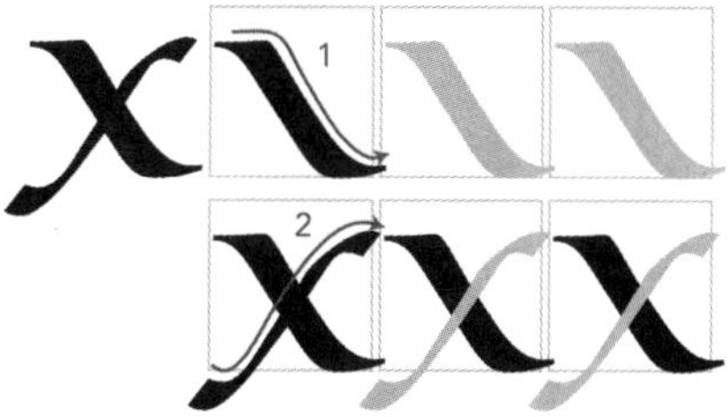

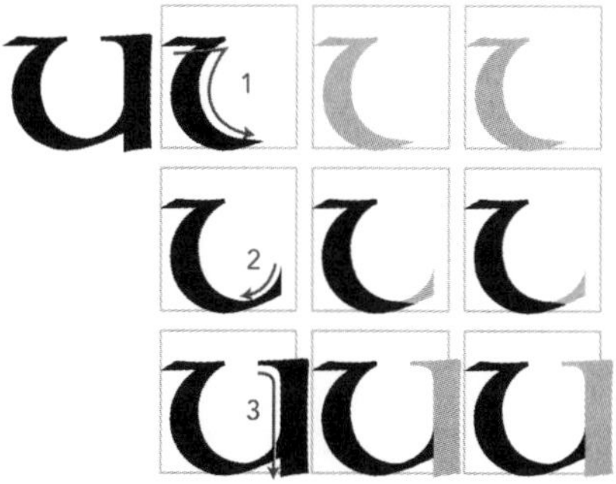

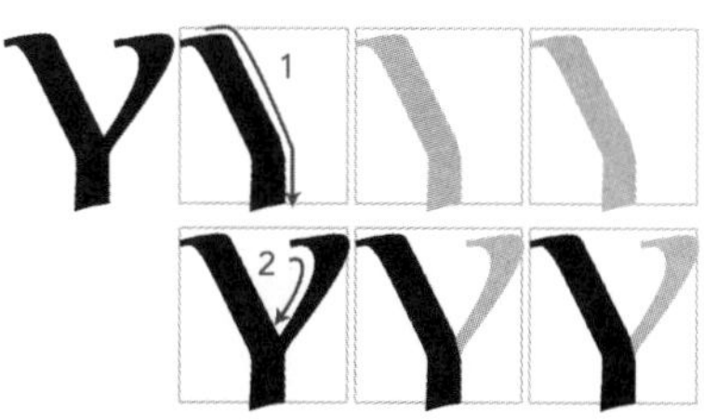

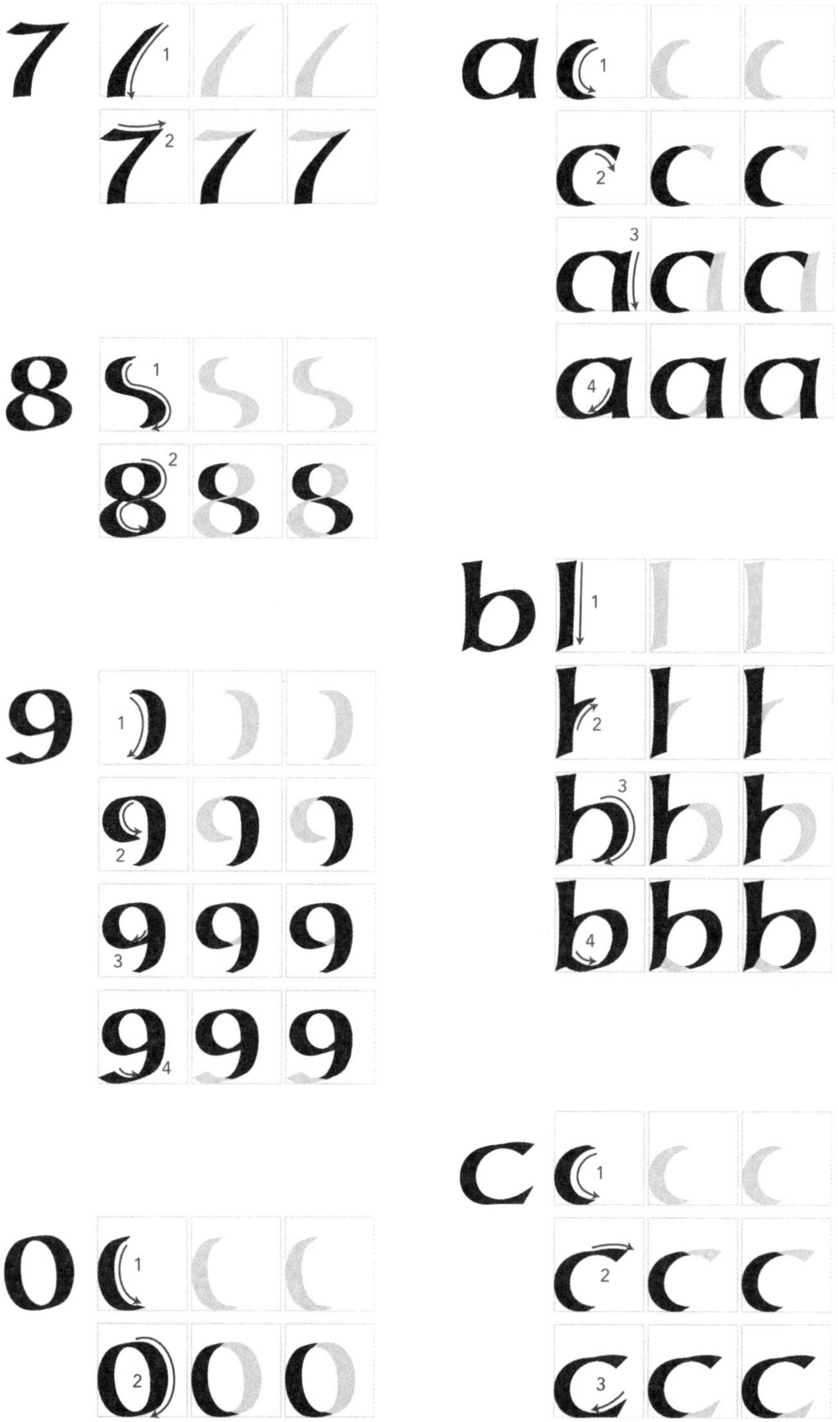
7
8
9
0
a
b
c

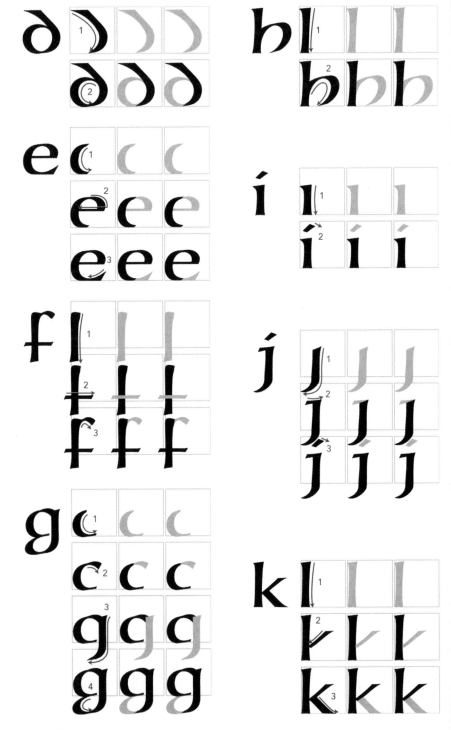

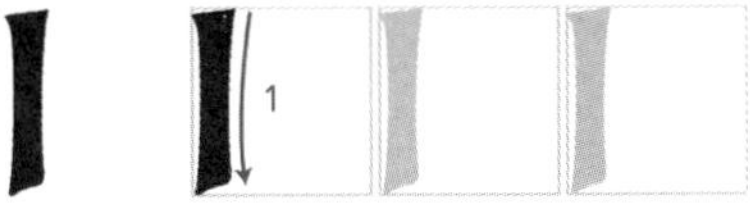
1

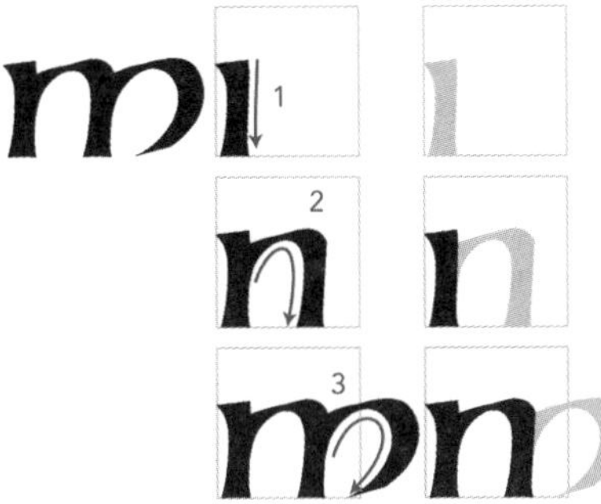
1
2
3

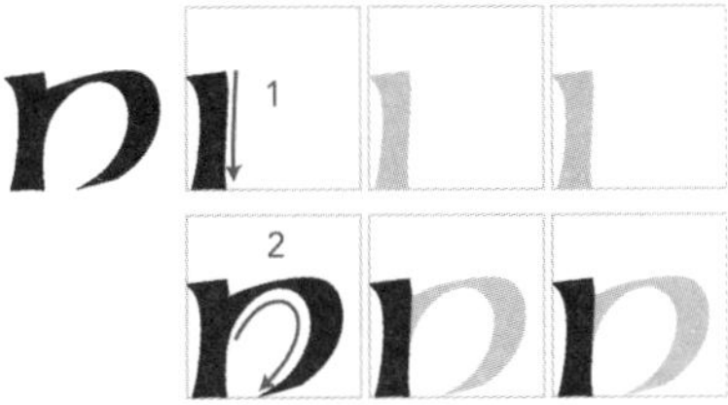
1
2

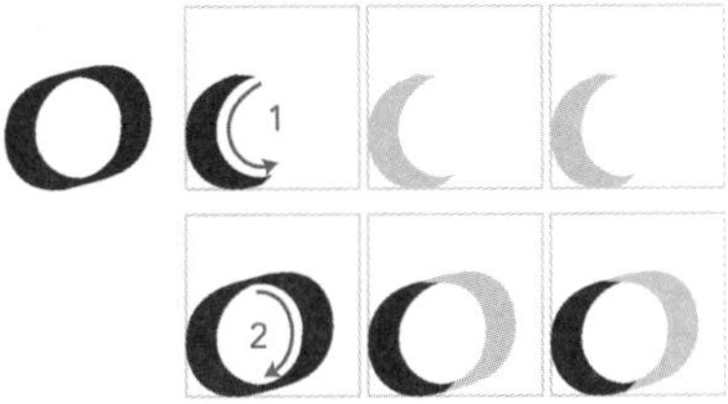
1
2

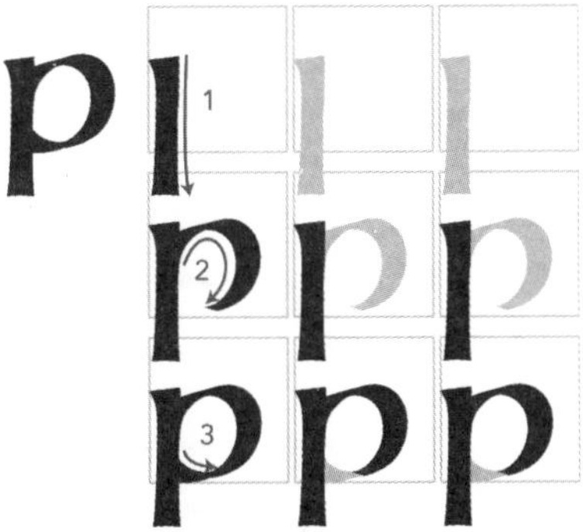
1
2
3

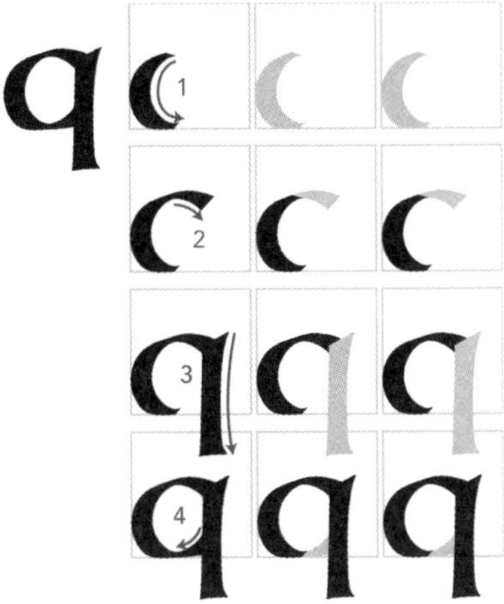
1
2
3
4

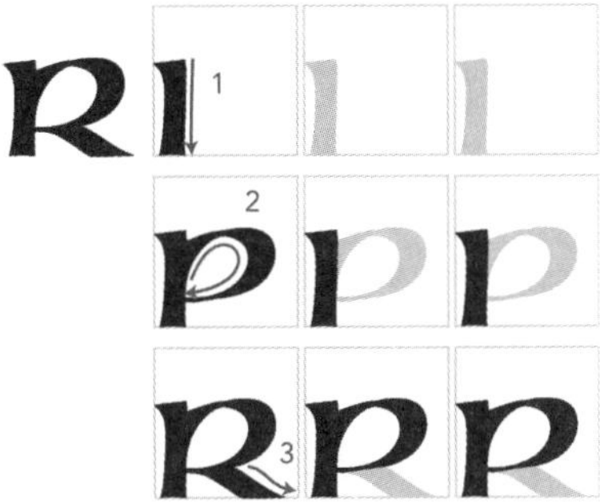
1
2
3

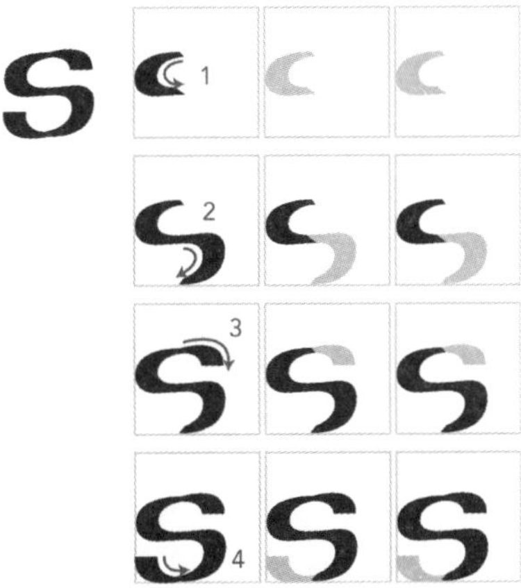
1
2
3
4

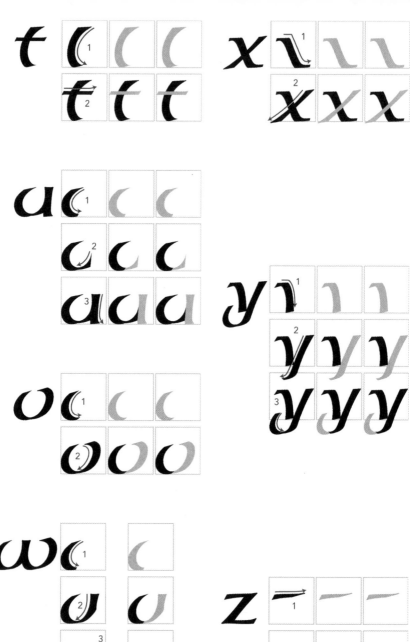
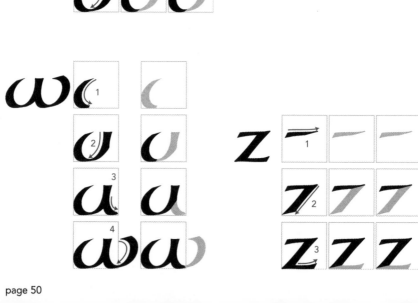

Gothic Alphabet

The Gothic alphabet was invented in the 4th century AD by Ulfilas, an Arian bishop, for translating the Bible into the Gothic language. The Gothic alphabet had 27 letters, 19 or 20 of which were derived from Greek uncial script, 5 or 6 modified slightly from Latin, and 2 either borrowed from runic script or invented independently. It is one of the most recognizable lettering styles in calligraphy and even though it looks very complicated, it is really one of the easiest styles of letters to create. Gothic letters are made from three basic strokes and one basic shape.

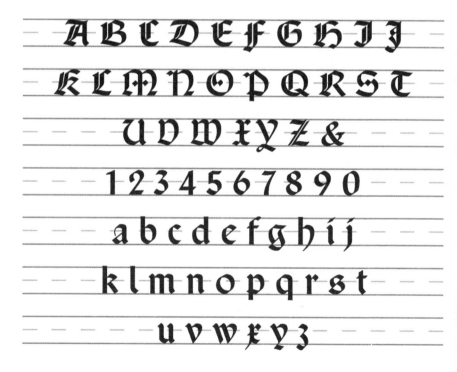

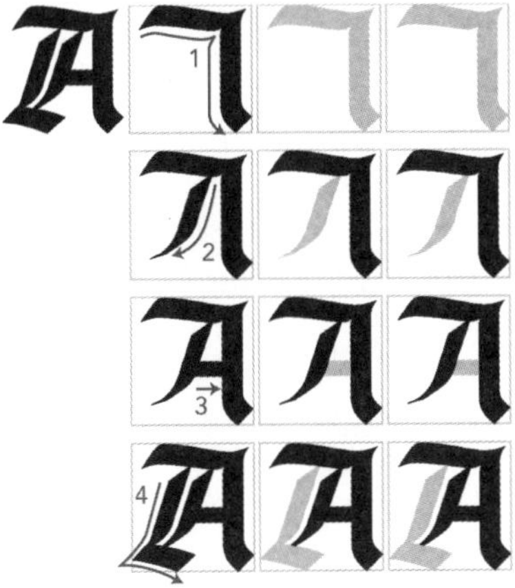
1
2
3
4

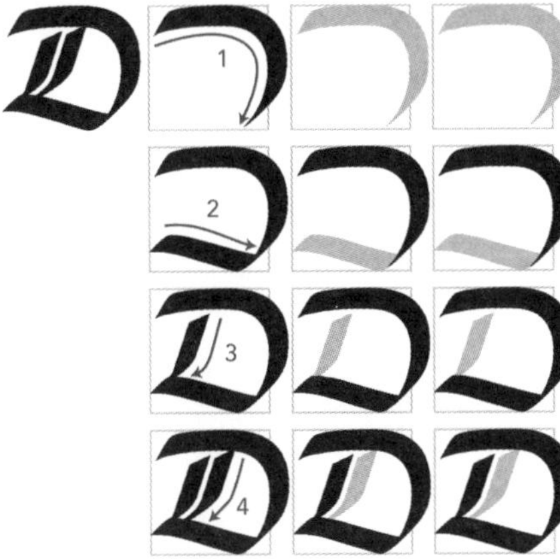
1
2
3
4

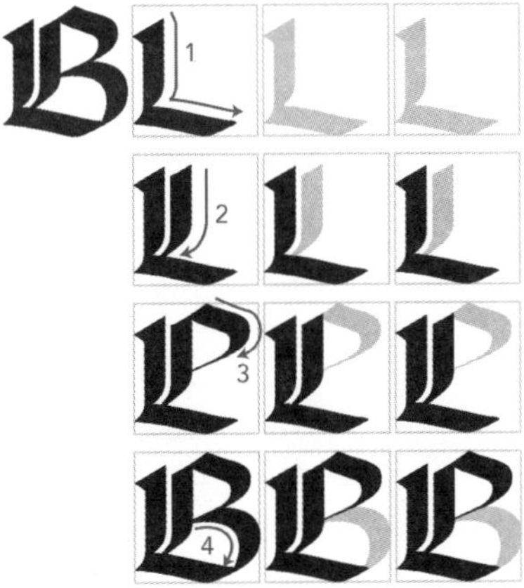
1
2
3
4

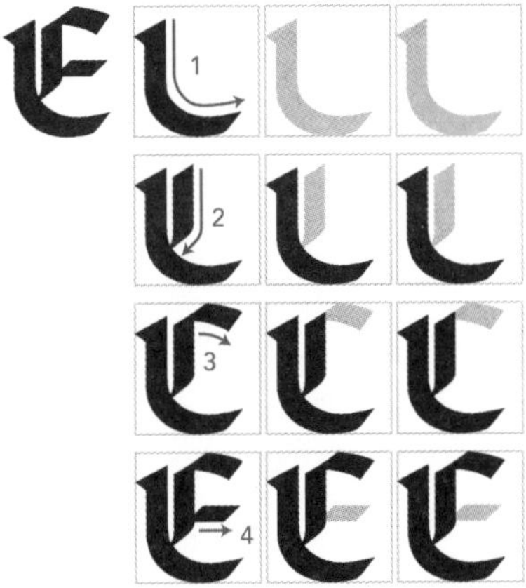
1
2
3
4

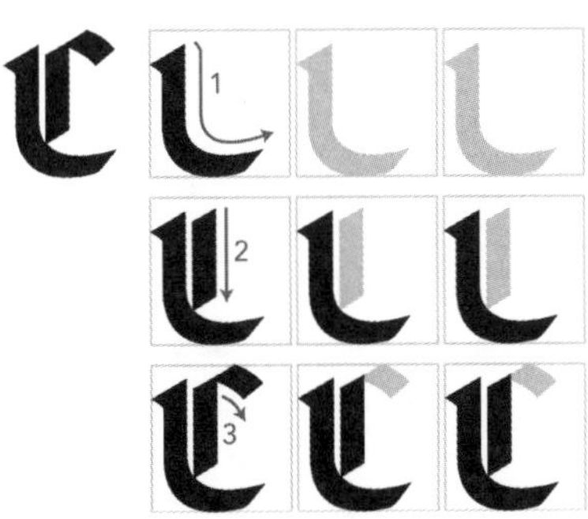
1
2
3

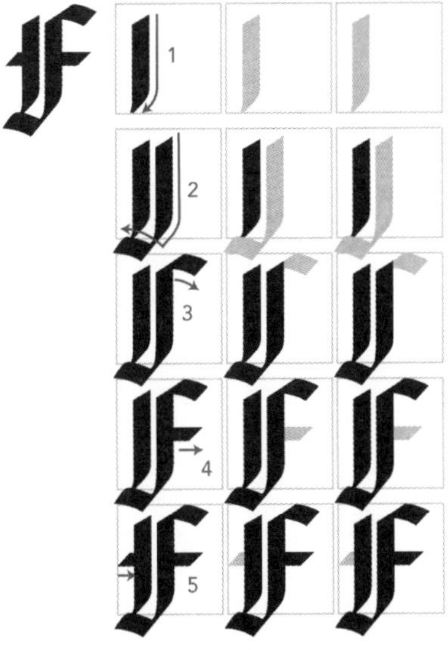
1
2
3
4
5

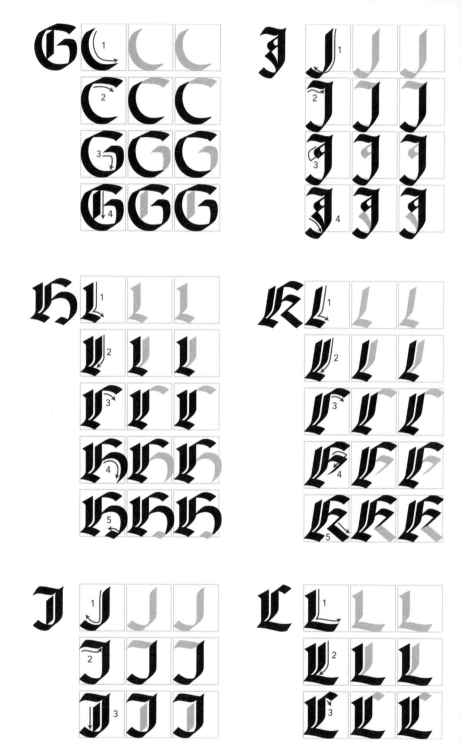

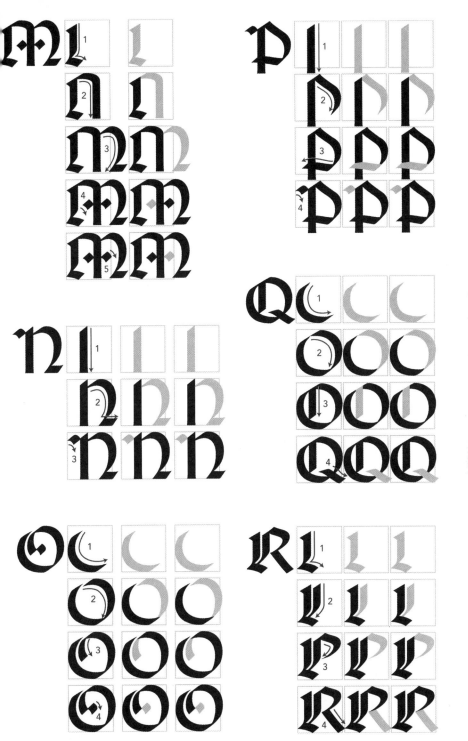

page 55

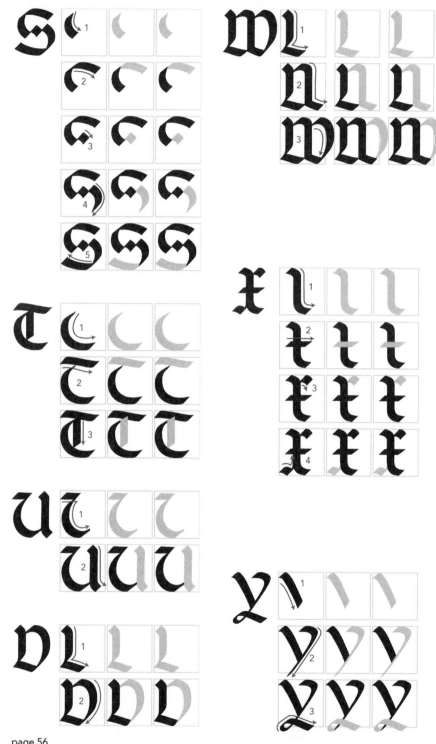

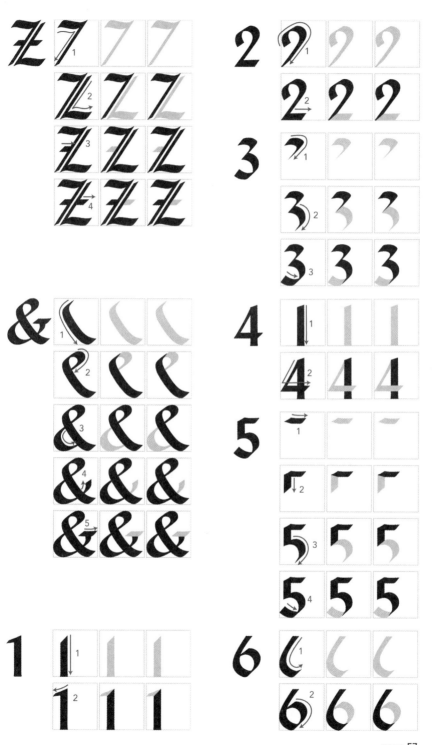

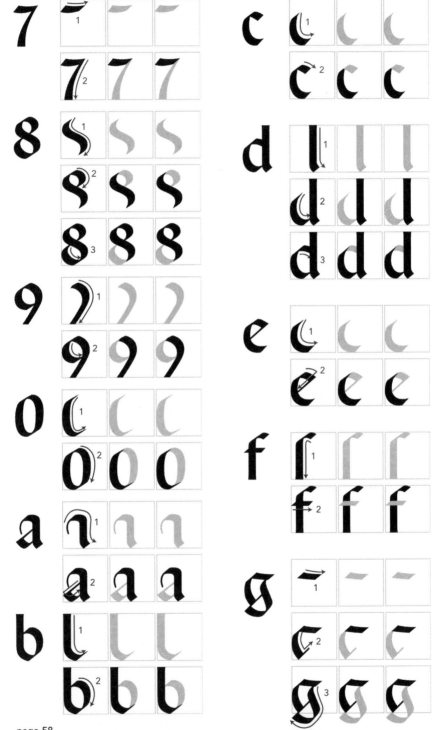

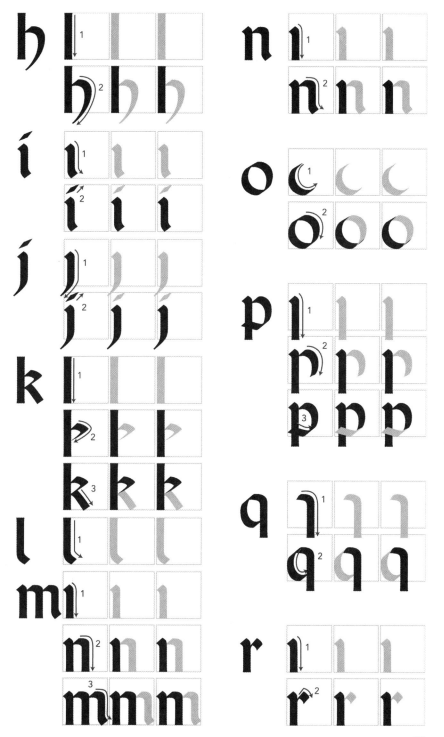

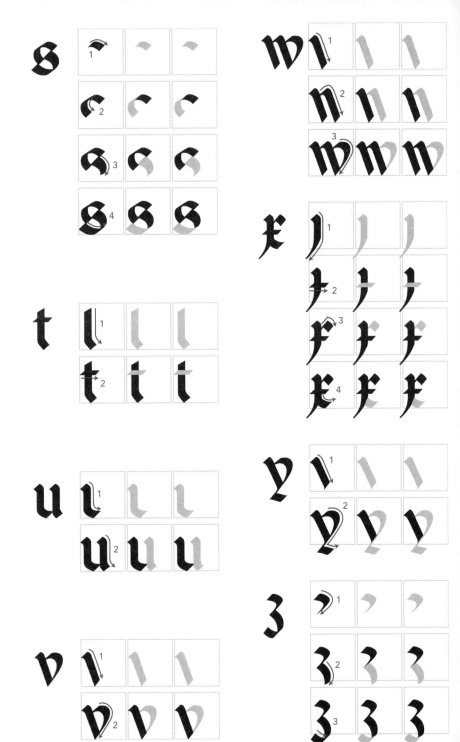

better

giggle

PLAY

Tasty

Smile

funky

DREAMS

FABULOUS

Happiness

wildest

Delight

relax fun

amuse

Celebration

Good

Laugh

adore

ENJOY

breathtaking

A B C D E
F G H I J
K L M N O
P Q R S T
U V
W X M
Y Z

CONTEMPORARY CALLIGRAPHY GRUNGE ALPHABET